God's Enrichment:
Birthing God's Riches

Lakisha Thomas Mitchell

ISBN: 978-1-7329549-0-8

DEDICATION

Firstly, let me give thanks to God for birthing this book out of me. He has been nothing but amazing to me. I never knew a book was in me until He revealed it. It's funny because I thought I knew myself until I met Him. Now I know a better and have become wiser me! I didn't write this book for me; I wrote this book for God. So, whatever and however, He plans to use it, it's up to Him. I'm just glad that I am the vessel He chose to bring it forth. Once again, God I bless you and I love you! Thank you for being DADDY! You will forever have my heart!

Secondly, I want to thank my husband Robert Mitchell for pushing me through this birthing processing. He gave me encouraging words when no one else was around to listen to me, and my manuscript thoroughly. My husband talked about my book when I wasn't talking about it. He had faith in this book as if he was the one writing it. I couldn't have asked for a better friend and husband. I must thank my babies; Lakendria Rose and Javarius Mitchell, you guys are the reason why I push so hard. I want to show you how to think big and outside of the box and that you can do anything that you put your minds to! I love you dearly.

Thirdly, I want to thank my mother and father. Those two are my biggest supporters. I'm so glad to call them my parents. Even though my mom doesn't say much, the smile on her face is louder than her actual words. I love you mom and keep smiling. You are a big sister to me. I thank you dad for your wisdom and prayers. You are not only my dad but also my friend! Your laughter and jokes warm my heart. Thank you for being an overflow in my life. I love you dad; you are the best.

Let's wrap this thing up by thanking my sister; she is my best friend, my cheerleader, my counselor, and my heart. There isn't another sister around that can top her. I say that from my heart. I would advise everyone to get them a Jackie! Finally, I want to thank my grandfather, Percy Thomas for his prayers and his love for God. If only you were here so I could ask you a million questions about your relationship with God! I hope you didn't forget to tell Jesus what I told you before you left this earth. I will never forget you. I love you to the moon and back. Thank you!

CONTENTS

Dedication iii

Introduction 1

1 You Are Worthy of His Plans 3

2 Giving Birth to Utterance 13

3 Divine Strength to Overcome and Push Out Greatness 19

4 Enriching the Spiritual Senses 27

5 Spiritual Enrichment through Prayer 37

About the Author 45

1 INTRODUCTION

In October 2019, I went on a forty-day fast which was a challenge for me. Towards the end of the fast, God revealed a book to me in my dreams that was titled "God's Enrichment." Let me start by explaining to you that I am not a person that reads a lot so I didn't think that I could ever write a book. I am what I call a scanner; I scan over books to get what I need and close them back up until I need them again.

As soon as my feet touched the floor the next morning, I began to write and write and write, until I was finished. After I finished writing the rough draft, I wanted to quit. I put the book down and didn't pick it back up until months after. Sounds crazy? You would think after writing the rough draft that it would be a smooth sailing afterwards, but not for me. See, God had already shown me the results of the completed book, but I had to push through the process in between the beginning and the end. That was the hardest part for me.

Birthing out your visions and dreams are not always easy, but the reward comes once they have manifested. What good is it if you just continue to dream and dream but never act on it? If God gives you a dream, He will make sure that it happens. He only needs you to act and follow through on what He has deposited in you.

I still can't believe it, this had to be God! There was a time I wanted to give up, but I kept saying that if God gave it to me, I was going to finish it. I went through a birthing process, and I can say that I'm finally finished. I would advise anyone not to give up on a dream. Birth your baby out! You can do it!

1 YOU ARE WORTHY OF HIS PLANS

Some people spend years trying to figure out their purpose in life. Often, people die with their dreams and visions locked inside of them because they didn't have any idea of how to make them manifest. There are people in prison because they have resorted to other means due to not knowing how to produce their passion in life. So many dreams and visions have died behind bars due to someone not having the knowledge of giving life to them.

The enemy has made it natural for us to think that we are unworthy to accomplish our dreams and visions by making us ignorant of our identity. Many a time, the enemy will use fear as a weapon to prevent God's visions from manifesting in your life. What fear does is that it keeps us in our comfort zones which prevents us from reaching out. **1 John 4:4** says, you have already won a victory over those people, because the Spirit who lives in you is greater than the spirit who lives in the world. As the world grows greater, we are to become greater also. Fear and ignorance will prevent you from seeing yourself greater than the world which will cause the world to always have dominion over you. Not seeing yourself how God sees you will keep you constantly defeated and make you live in perpetual fear. You should bear it in mind that you will always be greater than the world. You will always be greater than your circumstances.

God's Plans for You

God has a plan for you. **John 15:16** says, "you did not choose me. I chose you. I appointed you to go and produce lasting fruit, so that the Father will give you whatever you ask for, using my name." God chose us and gave us authority to produce and create new things. Sometimes, we are confronted with the problem of figuring out what our fruit is. So, let me help you with that because in the beginning, God gave us every seed-bearing plant on the face of the earth and every tree that has fruit with seed in it. God has enriched us with all kinds of seed-bearing ideas. Therefore, we can produce what we want, whenever we want. **Psalm 37:4** says, "take delight in the Lord, and He will give you the desires of your heart." You will always have thoughts and ideas to create new things because God has given it to you. You will always have seeds to sow because God has given it to you. We are favored to receive the desires of our hearts.

I have learned over the years that God will sometimes show you the outcome of a plan that He purposed for your life. The result looks great, but the challenge is taking the first step to make that vision or dream manifest physically. God will show you what is impossible to you but possible to Him. That's the beauty of using your faith. Your faith needs to be bigger than your vision to help manifest it without a tremendous struggle. You need to be stronger than your opponent to defeat him. **Mark 4:30-32** says, "What shall we say the kingdom of God is like, or what parable shall we use to describe it? It is like a mustard seed, which is the smallest of all seeds on earth. Yet when planted, it grows and becomes the largest of all garden plants, with such big branches that the birds can perch in its shade." Even though our ideas may seem small, when we act on them out of faith, God will cause them to grow so big until others will inquire about it. The greater the faith, the greater the visions become. Your faith activates and enhances your visons. In the upcoming chapters, I will explain how you can build your faith and gain strength to birth the invisible into the visible, and convert your visions into reality.

You Are Worthy of the Vision

The first step is knowing that you are worthy of the plan that God has for you. **Jeremiah 29:11** says, "I know the plans that I have for you, plans to prosper you and not harm you, plans to give you hope and a future." God promised us great things in life. At this very moment, we should be living and walking in greatness. God promised that we are the head, we are to lend to nations, and that everywhere our foot shall tread shall be ours. God declared that we shall multiply, we shall replenish, and we shall be blessed. **Genesis 1:28** says, "and God blessed them, and God said unto them be fruitful, and multiply, fill the earth, and subdue it." Let's break this down in simple terms. The word blessed means to favor. God favored man and then he gave man authority to be fruitful, which means to bring forth, create, invent or produce. God also gave man authority to multiply, which means He gave man the authority to increase and become greater. God gave man the power to make what he produces great and increase it to its maximum capacity in terms of number, width, or length. You have the ability to bring forth your dreams and multiply it into greatness.

When Adam and Eve disobeyed God's order in the garden, it cost them their glory which left them naked and afraid. In order to cover themselves, they had an idea to clothe their bodies with fig leaves. Most times when we think about Adam and Eve, we only talk about their sins and how they fell from glory. The plan of the enemy is for us to see our sins and not our greatness in Jesus. We have become so focused on Adam and

Eve's sins that it's hard for us to recognize their creativeness inventing clothes. God took their idea and made it greater by creating clothes out of animal skins for them. Sometimes, God needs us to act on an idea so that He can make it bigger and better. To this day, God is still giving us great ideas that continues to make Adam and Eve's invention better. Companies are making billions from Adams and Eve's idea. Adam and Eve were able to birth out their idea even through their failure. Not your failure, your sins nor your past disqualifies you from birthing out your dreams and visions. We must give God something to work with by initiating the vision. Your dreams should keep you up at night with excitement. Your visions should motivate you to wake up in the morning.

The second step is to believe in yourself. Knowing who you are in God plays a major role in believing in yourself. God called us out of Him and made us to become just like Him. God's spirit enriches us, making us powerful, creative, successful, and wealthy. "Enrichment" is defined as making something more meaningful, substantial, or rewarding. Enrichment is the act of making something more valuable. **Genesis 2:7** says, "the Lord God formed man from the dust of the ground and breathed into his nostrils the breath of life; and man became a living soul." God used clay, something that didn't initially have any value until it was shaped into something. Even though the clay laid there lifeless, as soon as God formed the dirt into man, it immediately had purpose which gave it value. God took His breath and breathed it into man which made man now one of the most valuable creations on earth. God's Spirit gives the soul and spirit eternal life and enriches the body that was made from dirt with the power of God. His Spirit makes us rich in every aspect of life.

The Bible says in **Proverbs 10:22**, "it is the blessing of the Lord that makes us rich." Everything about you is rich! We are created to live a prosperous in life! You are so valuable to God that He gave His Son for you to become great. The enemy will do anything to keep you feeling confused with negative thinking to keep your greatness suppressed. **John 10:10** says, "the thief's purpose is to steal and kill and destroy. My purpose is to give them a rich life and satisfying life." The enemy will still your dream and kill your vision in order to destroy your life. In all of this, it's important to know your worth. The benefit of this is that it keeps you motivated, keeps you moving and constantly striving for more. Knowing that God has planned a great life should keep you working hard and using your faith to obtain that abundant life that God has promised you.

The third and final thing is to "Just Do It". God has granted you power to produce wealth in every area of your life. There is power in our words. Faith and power in our words can make our lives to be heaven on earth. This means you don't have to die and go to heaven in order to get what God has for you. You don't have to die and go to heaven in order to become rich.

You don't have to wait until you get to heaven to become great and successful. You don't have to wait until you get to heaven to receive your promises. I hope you get my drift. The Word of God causes us to live a meaningful and fulfilled life through our adversities right here on earth.

Wisdom is Our Inheritance

In the beginning, God brought the animals before Adam and whatever he named them; they were so. He didn't have to consult with anyone. At Adam's words, that's what the animals were called. I can't say it loud and clear enough, your words carry weight! Some of us are still living off the words that our ancestors spoke years ago.

As children of God, we shall have whatever we say because of our inheritance through Jesus Christ. **Job 22:28** says, "you shall decree a thing, and it shall be established unto you." That means that whatever you decide, that's what it will be to you. If your decision is to be a multi-millionaire, then that's what you will be. If your decision is to own multi-businesses, then it will be so. Let the decree come out of your mouth! What's in you is waiting to come out.

God said in His word that "I knew you before you were in your mother's womb. God predestined you before the foundation of the world." You were never meant to be a cast out, a defeated fellow, a lost fellow, or an unfulfilled individual. **Revelations 5:12** says, "worthy is the Lamb, who was slain, to receive power, wealth and wisdom and strength and honor and glory and blessing." Because you are a joint heir to Christ, you inherited power, wealth, strength, honor, glory, and most importantly the blessing. This scripture tells us how wealthy we are in life at this very moment. Let me give you a glimpse of what God has in store for you.

- **Ephesians 1:13** says "In Him, you also, after listening to the message of truth, the gospel of your salvation – having also believed you were sealed with the **Holy Spirit of promise**

- **Psalm 112:3 Wealth and riches** *shall be* in his house: and his righteousness endureth forever.

- **Ecclesiastes 5:19** Every man also to whom God hath given **riches and wealth**, and hath given him power to eat thereof, and to take his portion, and to rejoice in his labour; this *is* the gift of God.

- **Ephesians 2:4** But God, who is **rich in mercy,** for his great love wherewith he loves us, Even when we were dead in sins, hath quickened us together with Christ, and hath raised *us* up together, and made *us* sit together in heavenly *places* in Christ Jesus: That in the ages to come he might shew the exceeding **riches** of

his grace in *his* kindness toward us through Christ
Jesus.

- **Deuteronomy 8:18** But remember the LORD your
  God, for it is he who gives you the **ability to
  produce wealth**, and so confirms his covenant,
  which he swore to your ancestors, as it is today.
- **Proverbs 8:18** With me **are riches and honor**,
  enduring **wealth and prosperity**

We are only able to access our inheritance fully by
faith. **Ephesians 1:3,** helps us to know that we are entitled to
all spiritual blessings that are stored in the heavenly realms.
When we believe in Christ Jesus, we are guaranteed an
inheritance of eternal blessings.

Ephesians 2:6, explains that God raised us up with
Christ and we are seated with him in heavenly realms. Realms
are defined as kingdoms, and this literally translates that we
are positioned in many different kingdoms in heaven. In order
to access the spiritual blessings in the heavenly places in Christ
Jesus, we need to learn how to speak the language.

As a veteran of the United States Army, my first
oversees duty assignment was in Kosovo. It was hard for me to
effectively communicate in Kosovo because I didn't speak or
understand the language. I had difficulty understanding the
simple things such as which restroom to use, because I couldn't

understand the writing on the door. It was difficult to get my laundry cleaned because I couldn't speak or understand their language. As it pertains to the Kingdom of God, in order to fully access everything in the Kingdom, we need to first learn the language and how the Kingdom works.

It's hard for us to receive or access the things of the Kingdom of God when we don't know how to speak the language of the kingdom. Whatever you believe, that's what you are to become. It is relevant to commune with God daily. Gaining a relationship with God gives you insight on knowing yourself. When communing with God, we get to exchange our intimate feelings for his intimate feelings. God says that He will give us beauty for ashes. When communing with God we get to share our intimate thoughts with Him, and He shares His intimate thoughts with us. **Mathew 4:4** says, "man shall not live by bread alone, but on every word that comes from the mouth of God." To enjoy a true, powerful, and worthy life, we need to read and hear God's word daily. **Jeremiah 15:16** says, "when I discovered your words, I devoured them. They are my joy and my heart's delight, for I bear your name, O LORD God of Heaven's Armies."

2 GIVING BIRTH TO UTTERANCE

The Bible makes us to understand in **Luke 1:26-35** that in the sixth month of Elizabeth's pregnancy, God sent the angel Gabriel to Nazareth, a town in Galilee, to a virgin pledged to be married to a man named Joseph, a descendant of David whose name was Mary. The angel went to her and said, "Greetings, you who are highly favored! The Lord is with you." Mary was greatly troubled at his words and wondered what kind of greeting this might be. But the angel said to her, "Do not be afraid, Mary; you have found favor with God. You will conceive and give birth to a son, and you are to call him Jesus. He will be great and will be called the Son of the Most High. The Lord God will give him the throne of his father David, and he will reign over Jacob's descendants forever; his kingdom will never end. "How will this be," Mary asked the angel, "since I am a virgin?" The angel answered, "The Holy Spirit will come on you, and the power of the Most High will overshadow you. So, the holy one to be born will be called the Son of God. Even Elizabeth your relative is going to have a child in her old age, and she who was said to be unable to conceive is in her sixth month. For no word from God will ever fail."

Fear is one of the main causes that may prevent you from birthing out the voice of God. It's natural to experience fear when doing something new, but you must not allow fear become a hindrance to birthing out your new reality. Fear will cause you to abort the seed that God has planted in you. You must remember that God has equipped you with everything that is needed to carry out the plan. God is not man that He should lie about his promises.

Another cause that will stop you from birthing out the voice of God is trying to have it figured out, the way or method God is going to do it. If it doesn't make sense to us, we have the tendency of casting down the promise. Even though the Angel greeted Mary as highly favored, she was still afraid of him. To Mary, the promise didn't make any sense and she tried to rationalize it with her natural senses. Mary immediately began to question the Angel by asking how is was going to be possible since she was a virgin. God isn't interested in your present condition. The more reason why God did choose Mary was because of her present condition. God doesn't care that it's never been done before. He's ready to break protocol on your behalf. God only needs you to say yes to the promise. God is a supernatural God and He operates by the supernatural.

The Bible says in **1 Corinthians 1:5** that in everything you were enriched in Him, in all **UTTERANCE** and all **KNOWLEDGE**. The word "utterance" in this verse is translated from the Hebrew word logos. It means of speech: a word, uttered by a living voice which embodies a conception or idea. God's word is rich, and His word is in you. People fail to see their dreams come true because they are looking for handouts or help, when what they need is already in them. Open your mouth and release God's word for your life. God's word will bring you out of failure; it will bring you out of being that mediocre state and it will bring you into success.

In the beginning, God furnished the world with His words. God called forth light with a word. He called forth the land, the sky, the heavens and earth with the spoken word of His mouth. He then told the waters to bring forth a swarm of moving creatures and flying creatures that may fly above the earth. God also said, "let the earth bring forth living creatures after his kind." When God spoke a prophetic word to the land, the sky, and the waters; they all had to act as a womb to give birth to what was spoken to them. When God was done furnishing every area of the earth with His utterance, He looked at it and declared it good. You have the same authority to speak and furnish your own life just as God furnished the earth. God has given you the power to arrange and rearrange your life. If you don't like the way your life is going, change it! If you don't like the furniture in your house, you change it, right? We even rearrange our furniture when it gets old to us. You can do the same to your life. You have authority over what, when, where and how to produce or eliminate anything in your life.

Your mind is a womb where ideas and thoughts are conceived; it's your job to birth out these ideas and thoughts that are given by the Holy Spirit. We often have a hard time recognizing if our ideas and thoughts are from God. Through my experience, it has become easy to recognize an idea or thought from God by knowing my own thought process. The thought becomes an unction, and it feels rich in my mind

The word "knowledge" in 1 Corinthians 1:5 is translated from the Hebrew word gnosis. It means general intelligence, a deeper more perfect and enlarged knowledge, and understanding. Seeking God from a spiritual place helps you understand His language and become familiar with his voice. God says, His sheep will know His voice. Trust me; you will know when God is speaking to you. God will speak to you in dreams concerning your future. God will give you visions about your future. God will cause a person to prophesy to you about your future. I like to look at it this way, anything that goes against my mind or is too big of a thought for me, is usually God speaking to me.

The book of **Habakkuk 2:1-3** says, "I will stand upon my watch, and set me upon the tower, and I will watch to see what he will say unto me, and what I shall answer when I am reproved. And the Lord answered me and said, write the vision, and make it plain upon the tables, that he may run that reads it. For the vision is yet for an appointed time, but at the end it shall speak, and not lie though it tarry, wait for it; because it will surely come, it will not tarry." Whatever God gives to you, write it down plainly so that it will come to pass. It is best to keep a journal or even create a vision board of the visions that God has given to you. The scripture says that at the right time, what you wrote down will happen. He that reads it will run, which means he should move quickly to call out what he read. Even though your vision is at an appointed time, it's coming quickly. It's in a hurry to manifest!

3 DIVINE STRENGTH TO OVERCOME AND PUSH OUT GREATNESS

Samson was a man that was born with an unusual amount of strength. His strength developed as he grew, and he defeated obstacles that a normal person couldn't overcome without any help. It wasn't until Samson lost his strength that he had to rely on God for divine strength. Sometimes you may lose strength after fighting many battles, but God's word has said that His grace is sufficient for you, for His power is made perfect in weakness. The word "power" in this verse is translated from the Hebrew word dunamis. It has a few definitions that I would like to share with you.

1. Strength power, ability

A. inherit power, power residing in a thing by

virtue of its nature,

B. power of performing miracles;

C. the power and influence which belongs to riches and wealth.

The book of **Ephesians 1:20-21** says, "That power is the same mighty strength he exerted when he raised Christ from the dead and seated him at the right hand in the heavenly realms, far above all rule and authority, power and dominion, and every name that is invoked, not only in the present age but also in the one to come." God has given us incomparable strength to run and finish this race of life. The strength that we possess outweighs our adversary's strength. The strength of the enemy doesn't compare to God's strength.

The enemy will try to take away our vision so as to stop us from seeing our future. **Proverbs 29:18** says, "where there is no vision, the people perish." Samson couldn't physically see due to his eyes being gouged out, but God endowed Him with strength to finish the assignment. So even when it looks like we are defeated, we should bear in mind that we are still victorious. Although when we can't physically see the outcome, it still doesn't stop God from showing up and giving us great victory.

I preached on birthing out the promises of God at a few different churches. Every time I preached the sermon, I received and witnessed amazing testimonies. While preaching the sermon for the second time, I told the people that God was healing some of them so that they could give birth to ministries. After the service that night, one older lady said to me that during the sermon, her stomach began to burn (which I had heard a few times after preaching on birthing). The lady said she couldn't have any more kids, so she wasn't sure why her stomach was burning. She said that after I prayed for her, she received an instant healing in her back from over a 20-year nerve condition in her back and hip that left her using crutches at times. The lady said that she had a ministry inside of her that needed to be birthed out. Her testimony reminded me of how God healed Sarah's old dead body in order to birth Isaac into the earth. Whatever God must do to get his plan into the earth, He is willing to do it; He's just looking for an available womb to use.

Name Your Vision

Every time that God was ready to bring His promise into the earth, He named it. When God was ready to bring Jesus into the earth, He told Mary that the name of the holy thing she was going to carry will be called Jesus. When God was ready to bring Isaac into the earth, He named him. When

God was ready to bring John into the world, He named Him. Every child that is born into this world has a name. Put a name on what God has given you to birth out. Listen carefully because God will sometimes give you a name for the vision just as He did with Isaac, Jesus, and John.

Sadly, to say, there are people that may be overdue with visions, dreams, promises and even multi-million-dollar thoughts and ideas. I declare after reading this book that every dream and idea, and thought that has been deposited in your mind by the Holy Spirit will be birthed out. You are designed to give birth! You are designed to be fruitful! You are designed to multiply.

God would not give you a vision or dream if He knew you couldn't accomplish it. In Christ you can do all things even if it looks like anything isn't going in your favor. **Mark 11:23,** says that everything is possible for one who believes. The word "possible" in this verse is translated from the Hebrew word dunatos. The word possible means:

1. Able, powerful, mighty, and strong

    a. Mighty in wealth and influence

    b. Strong in soul- To bear calamities and trials with fortitude and patience

2. To be able (to do something)

    a. Mighty, excelling in something

    b. Having power for something.

Believing gives you the ability, power, the might, and the strength to do His will. The bigger the dream, the greater the birth pains. You must realize that you have the strength to excel in everything that you are set out to do. You are not meant to die with purpose locked up inside of you. In the book of

Matthew, one of the fig tree's purposes was to feed Jesus. Jesus walked up to the fig tree looking for its fruit, but because the fig tree wouldn't produce out of the world's season, it ends up dying with purpose in it. The fig tree dies with seeds, fruits and more life locked in it. The fig tree ends up dying with riches in it. God didn't design you to be like the fig tree. God made you like Him. You have the power to produce at any time. You have the power to produce anything. You don't have to wait on the world to tell you when to start a business or where you can birth your dreams. Like the fig tree, everyone including Kings are looking for your fruit, but unlike the fig tree, you don't have to wait on timing to produce fruit. **Psalm 1:3** says that we are like trees planted along the riverbank, bearing fruit in each season. Their leaves never wither, and they prosper in all they do. Jesus is our source and He causes us to flourish in everything that we do.

You Can Give Birth at Anytime

You have authority over time and you are allowed to operate at any time as long as you have the faith required. When Mary and Jesus were at a party that ran out of wine, Mary caused Jesus to create a miracle out of His timing. Jesus told Mary that it wasn't His time, but Mary told the servants to do whatever He told them to do. I like to think of it as Mary's words grew legs of faith and walked into the future and brought time into her right now. Immediately, Jesus began to work a miracle all because of Mary's faith. Your faith keeps you in control of your future. Jesus turned water into wine all because of faith. When you let faith do its job, Jesus will turn your nothing into something, your little into a lot, and your dreams into manifestations!

The bigger the vision, the harder you will have to push. That means your level of strength needs to be bigger than your dreams. Sometimes you will face obstacles that are made to strengthen you for a great dream. Look at David for example, he had to fight a bear, a lion, and Goliath. David did not know that his fights were preparing him to be a king. Your fights have prepared you for where you are right now. Your fights have prepared you to stand before great men and women. Your fights in life have prepared you to stand in great positions. You have been strengthened for this very moment!

Divine strength guarantees victory in our everyday lives if we are determined not to give up and this is the strength that we have in Jesus Christ. Just when the enemy thought they had taken away Samson's strength, God enriched him with a power that the enemy could not take away. Samson was able to tear down and destroy the enemy in its own camp. You also have the power to destroy the enemy wherever you are at this time. You may be at a dead-end job or a dead-end place, but you have the power to change where you are currently. Don't look at changing your situation as being stressful. Anything that's outside your normal can be stressful. I've asked God to help me know the difference between hard work and stress. I want to work hard at everything that I do, especially for the Kingdom of God. I know your mind and body may not be familiar with hard work which will cause you to think you are stressed out, but don't fuss. Feeling stressed could make you quit or give up easily. To get where you need to be will sometime cause you to work hard, but yield a bountiful reward in the long run.

4 ENRICHING THE SPIRITUAL SENSES

Now, faith is the assurance (title deed, confirmation) of things hoped for (divinely guaranteed), and the evidence of things not seen [the conviction of their reality-faith comprehends as fact what cannot be experienced by the physical senses]. **Hebrews 11:1 AMP**

Let's deal with faith! We live in a sense making world; where everything must make sense or needs to be in order for things to happen. We are from a Kingdom where things do not need to make sense for it to work. The bible records the story of a man who was born blind. Jesus spat on the ground and made mud, then Jesus put some of the mud on the eyes of the blind man and told him to go wash it off in the Siloam pool. After the man washed himself, he was able to see. To the natural mind, that doesn't make any sense, but in our kingdom, anything is possible with Jesus Christ.

My grandfather would heal people suffering from asthma by putting them in a chimney with ashes. Even though that doesn't make any sense, but he was an anointed man that God used as a vessel to heal His people. He would do what was considered abnormal to the world but normal in the kingdom of God. As I can recalled it worked every time! **2 Corinthians 5:7** says, "We walk by faith and not by sight." The scripture lets us know that we are not to operate by our sight or our five senses. Our faith gives us the ability to see spiritually what we can't see naturally. The stronger the faith, the bigger the vision becomes. In the book of John, God told Nathaniel that because he believes greater things he will see. Our belief in God gives us confidence and our confidence bring us great reward. **John 14:12** says that if we believe in Him greater things shall we do. Hold tight to your confessions; hold tight to your dreams and promises. God told Jacob that He would not leave him until He had done what He had promised to him. That same promise is given to us. God will finish in you what He has started; just don't give up.

Sometimes, what we see naturally can deter us from birthing out our dreams and visions. We as humans have five basic senses: touch, sight, hear, smell, and taste. It is important to understand and that we have five senses in the realm of the spirit, just as well as we have them in the physical. It is necessary that you use your spiritual senses to help navigate and function in this world. The scripture makes it plain when it says we walk by faith and not by sight. That immediately puts our natural five senses in the back seat. Let's take a quick look **Genesis 27:12-27,** which shows how our natural senses could fail us at any given time.

Genesis 27: 12-27

What if my father touches me? He'll see that I'm trying to trick him, and then he'll curse me instead of blessing me." But his mother replied, "Then let the curse fall on me, my son! Just do what I tell you. Go out and get the goats for me!" So Jacob went out and got the young goats for his mother. Rebekah took them and prepared a delicious meal, just the way Isaac liked it. Then she took Esau's favorite clothes, which were there in the house, and gave them to her younger son, Jacob. She covered his arms and the smooth part of his neck with the skin of the young goats. Then she gave Jacob the delicious meal, including freshly baked bread. So Jacob took the food to his father. "My father?" he said. "Yes, my son," Isaac answered. "Who are you— Esau or Jacob?" Jacob replied, "It's Esau, your firstborn son. I've done as you told me. Here is the wild game. Now sit up and eat it so you can give me your blessing." Isaac asked, "How did you find it so quickly, my son?" "The LORD your God put it in my path!" Jacob replied. Then Isaac said to Jacob, "Come closer so I can touch you and make sure that you really are Esau." So, Jacob went closer to his father, and Isaac touched him. "The voice is Jacob's, but the hands are Esau's," Isaac said. But he did not recognize Jacob, because Jacob's hands felt hairy just like

Esau's. So, Isaac prepared to bless Jacob. "But are you really my son Esau?" he asked. "Yes, I am," Jacob replied. Then Isaac said, "Now, my son, bring me the wild game. Let me eat it, and then I will give you my blessing." So Jacob took the food to his father, and Isaac ate it. He also drank the wine that Jacob served him. Then Isaac said to Jacob, "Please come a little closer and kiss me, my son." So Jacob went over and kissed him. And when Isaac caught the smell of his clothes, he was finally convinced, and he blessed his son. He said, "Ah! The smell of my son is like the smell of the outdoors, which the LORD has blessed!

In this passage, all natural five senses were used physically, every sense failed Isaac but his hearing. His own senses not only failed him, but also caused him to give away his oldest son's blessing. Even though it was Isaac's, reality it was still a false reality. Sometimes, relying on your physical senses can cause you to miss what God has for you. The enemy has a sure way of creating stumbling blocks when your spiritual senses are not in use. If Isaac was able to use his spiritual senses, he wouldn't have been tricked by his own son. Your spiritual senses should be used primarily to function in the spiritual and physical realm. Let's take a look at our five senses versus our spiritual senses.

Seeing

The Bible makes us to understand in **2 King 6: 15-17**

that when the servant of the man of God got up and went out early the next morning, an army with horses and chariots had surrounded the city. "Oh no, my lord! What shall we do? The servant asked. "Don't be afraid," the prophet answered. "Those who are with us are more than those who are with them." And Elisha prayed, "Open his eyes, Lord, so that he may see." Then the Lord opened the servant's eyes and looked and saw the hills full of horses and chariots of fire all around Elisha.

Here, Elisha and his servant were looking at the same thing but from two different realms. Elisha could see in the natural and spiritual realm and the servant could only see in the natural realm, which cause them to see from two different perspectives. The servant could only see from a defeated standpoint which was in the natural realm. Only being able to see in the natural realm caused the servant to lose before the battle even started. Before the servant eyes were opened to the spiritual realm, he could only see defeat, but when his eyes were opened in the spiritual realm, he was able to see victory. Sometimes, we are so focused on what we see in our everyday lives that we forget or ignore the vision that God has shown us.

Touching

One day, while I was in the bathroom praying with my hands lifted in the air, it felt as if someone put gloves on both of my hands. After that, I began to feel a powerful anointing on my hands every time I opened my mouth to pray. It was so powerful that when I jumped up and down, I could feel the power on my hands even when I wasn't talking about God. I could simply be thinking about him and then the anointing would come upon my hands. Soon after, I realized that I was able to feel and sense things spiritually through my hands. What do I mean by that? I realized that when I would get around someone that is sick, sad or just having a bad day, my hands would have an irritating burning sensation. Sometimes the burning sensation would intensify until I ask the person what is going on with them.

I've had times when a lot of people were hugging or touching me, and my hands started to have that irritating burning sensation. When this happens, I usually ask myself who touched me just to see if I could identify who was either sick or just going through a tough time at that moment. My senses were so heightened even to the point that it seemed awkward to sit by someone because I didn't want to feel or know what they were going through. In the natural realm, it would be difficult to pick up people's emotions just by sitting beside them, but because my spiritual senses are at work, it's easier to pick up on their emotions.

Hearing

I recall being at the altar one Sunday, praying for someone and when I touched the person, I could hear the word "school" but I didn't literally hear it through my ears, more like I heard it through my hands. I asked the young lady if she was in school, and she said yes. After that day, I realized that I could hear spiritually through my hands.

On another day, I was praying for a man when I realized that I felt a lump move from one part of his stomach to the other. When I asked the man if he did feel the lump, he told me no, but that it was the side of his stomach where he was experiencing pain that he hadn't told anyone about. The man told me that after

I prayed for him, he was healed instantly. I have experienced so many other occasions where I could feel things moving in people's body that they couldn't feel. **Hab 3:4** says, "His splendor was like the sunrise; rays flashed from his hand, where his power was hidden." It's funny now, that my hands have literally become my ears.

Smelling

Our sense of smell is important. Just like we can smell something naturally and tell if its rotten; we also can smell rotten things in the spiritual realm. Our sense of smell is one senses that God uses to get out attention. When I got baptized in the Holy Spirit, my sense of smell definitely heightened. I could smell demons in my sleep. Sometimes, God would use the smell of something burning to wake me up in the middle of the night so he could talk to me. Just like we can walk in the room and tell who has been there because of the scent of their cologne, or their natural scent; we should be able to tell who has been in the room because of their spiritual scent also. **2 Corinthians 2:15** says, "For we are like a sweet-smelling incense offered by Christ to God, which spreads among those who are being saved and those who are being lost." We should develop our sense of smell to sense things spiritually.

Tasting

The Bible says in **Psalm 38:4** "Taste and see that the

Lord is good; blessed is the one who takes refuge in him." The word "taste" in the Hebrew is taw-am which means to eat. **Mathew 4:4** says, "Man shall not live by bread alone, but every word that proceeds out of the mouth of God." God told Ezekiel to eat the scroll and to fill his stomach with it and Ezekiel said the scroll tasted like honey for sweetness.

We must understand that we are to have whatever we desire in the earth; and to do so, we must have faith in the promises of God. The Bible makes us to understand in **John 14** that whatever we ask in His name, He will do it. God is waiting on us to ask for what we want! We are not to let our everyday lives get in the way of the promises of God. God has already made provisions for us, even when it doesn't look like it. Your spiritual senses help you not only to do God's work, but also to live a favorable life. It will help you make the right business decision, take the correct path, get involved with the right individual and so forth.

5 SPIRITUAL ENRICHMENT THROUGH PRAYER

Prayer enriches us by strengthening the muscles of our inner man. The more we pray, the stronger we become mentally, emotionally, physically, and spiritually. We can win any battle that comes against us through prayer. Prayer is a key that opens us up to the realm of the spirit.

One day, while I was in prayer with my eyes closed, I felt a presence pass by me all of a sudden. I could feel the wind from its presence, and I could see the shadow even though my eyes were closed. At the time, it startled me because it was my first time ever encountering the presence of the supernatural. I've learned now to expect to encounter the supernatural every day. Prayer can activate our five senses in the spiritual realm, which I talked about in **Chapter 4.** Prayer gives you access to get into and operate in the spiritual realm. Through prayer, you can tune in on the same frequency as the Kingdom of Heaven.

Through prayer, you can understand and know what God wants to do in the earth and in your life. I have firsthand seen a woman's leg grow an inch right before my eyes, because of prayer. If prayer can grow a leg back, imagine what it can do in your life.

What is Prayer

Prayer is a communication system between man and God. It is a spiritual translation from heaven to earth and from earth to heaven. It is important to know and understand the Word of God, as it helps to release the power of God through prayer in the earth realm more effectively. The Bible says in **Ephesians 6:18 KJV**, "Praying always with all prayer and supplication in the Spirit, being watchful to this end with all perseverance and supplications for all saints." Right from the beginning of times, we have been given authority and dominion over the earth and every creeping thing on the earth. The Word of God released through prayer breaks down barriers and limitations in our lives, cities, states, countries, and nations. Every believer has the right and the privilege to pray with boldness and authority. Prayer is a key to helping us get our visions and dreams birthed on the earth. The Bible says in **Jude 1:20** "build yourselves up in this most holy faith by praying in the Holy Spirit." With this in mind, we are to position ourselves to grow in the Kingdom of God. Praying in the Holy Spirit helps us to hear and understand the ways of the Kingdom.

As a child, during the hot summer months in a small town in Louisiana, my grandfather would round up all the kids in the community to hand pick peas. Around noon, when the temperature would have gone over 100 degrees, it would be so hot that we could barely finish the job. In the midst of the heat, my grandfather would make everyone pause and bow their heads. He would pray to God for the wind to blow to help cool us off. By the time my grandfather finished praying, the wind would begin to blow. As a child, it amazed me so much until one hot summer day, I decided to do the same, but when I prayed, nothing happened. As I got older, I realized that not only did my grandfather have a relationship with the Father, he also knew his position as a child of God. The Bible says in **Hebrews 11:6**, "The man that approaches God must know that He is", (He must know both that God IS and He, the believer Is).

As a believer, it is important to know that we are authorized and worthy to be in the presence of God. The Bible says in **Hebrews 4:16**, "Let us therefore come boldly unto the throne of grace." Knowing that you are authorized to be in His presence makes you more confident and comfortable to come boldly to the throne of God.

Praying the Word of God gives us automatic and

successful results. The Bible says in **Matthew 16:19**, "I will give you the keys of the kingdom of heaven, and whatever you bind on earth will be bound in heaven, and whatever you lose on earth will be loosed in heaven." Heaven is waiting on you! To bind means "to restrict, stop, hinder, fetter, check, hold back, arrest, or put to stop to. To lose means to untie, unbind, unlock, liberate, release, forgive, or free. Keys give you the authority to bind and loose. While praying, it is important to use the right scripture for the situation at hand. It simply does you no bit of good to have a set of keys that does not open or lock the door to a room. We must use the right scripture to get the right results. Heaven will not and cannot do what we will not give it permission to do.

Having faith in God and yourself is a key factor in this stage of the prayer. You need to have confidence that God has heard and delivered you. You also need to have confidence that you belong to the commonwealth of Zion and that you have the right to ask for the things that you need. The Bible says in **John 14:13**, "And I will do whatever you ask in my name, so that the Father may be glorified in the Son. You may ask me for anything in my name, and I will do it."

Prayer connects us to the Heavens. Prayer can release the fire and power of God, command our mornings, enlarge our territories, root out, releases, overthrow, and etc. Prayer protects us from the things that are seen and unseen and from the plot and schemes of the enemy. Prayer breaks generational curses, ungodly soul ties, and ungodly covenants. In **Genesis 1:26**, the Bible says, "Let Us make man in Our image, according to Our likeness; let them have dominion over the fish of the sea; over the birds of the air, and over the cattle, over all the earth and over every creeping thing that creeps on the earth." God gave us the authority and ability to live successful lives and to make our lives here on earth reflect Heaven. When the serpent deceived Eve, it interfered with the plan that God had initially. God cursed the serpent, telling it that "because you have done this you are cursed." When the enemy is trying to interfere in our lives, we have the power to pray to stop the plan of the enemy.

The Bible says in **Jude 1:20**, "But you, beloved, building yourselves up on the most holy faith, praying in the Holy Spirit." As believers, we are responsible for confessing and professing the word of God. Our faith in ourselves and God should produce what we need to live this life successfully. The Bible says in **Hebrews 10:23**, "He who promised is faithful." It's in the place of prayer that we can birth what God has placed inside of us. In **Isaiah 66:8**, the Bible says, "shall I bring to the moment of birth and not give delivery. Or shall I who gives delivery shut the womb." God is not a god that will give you a dream and then cause you to abort it. God is not a god that will give you a dream and then kill your womb so that you can't give birth. God will deposit a vision or dream in you and then become a midwife and help you give birth to it. That's the type of God you serve! He will be your Husband one minute and deposit a seed in your womb and then become a Midwife the next minute to help you give birth to the seed.

Prayer gives us access to our future which is our right now in God. Prayer gives us access into the spiritual realm, to see the divine promises of God. In **Act 9,** the Bible makes us to understand that Saul was blinded by an encounter that he had with God. Then God told a disciple named Ananias, saying "go inquire of a man named Saul for behold, he is praying. And in a vision has seen a man named Ananias coming in and putting his hand on him, so that he might receive his sight." Saul was physically blind, but because he was praying, it activated his eyesight in the realm of the spirit. Prayer will cause you to see light in dark places, prayer will cause you to see life in dead places. Saul was able to see his breakthrough, healing, and deliverance in the spirit realm because of prayer. Prayer is a powerful tool that is needed so that you can see yourself travail and give birth.

My Prayer for you:

I release the power of God over your life. I declare the anointing of God to destroy every stronghold, ungodly soul tie and ungodly thought in your life. I release the spirit of life, joy, well-being, wealth, and prosperity into your life in the name of

Jesus. I declare that you are the righteousness of God (2 Corinthians 5:21). I declare that you are victorious in Christ (1 Corinthians 15:57). I declare that you are redeemed in Christ (Romans 3:24). I declare that you have liberty in Christ (Galatians 2:4). I declare that you are whole and complete in Christ (Colossians 2:10). I declare that you can do all things through Christ who strengthens you (Philippians 4:13). I declare that God shall supply all of you need through Christ (Philippians 4:19). I declare that I you are a new creature in Christ (2 Corinthians 5:17). I declare that you are walking in your divine inheritance. I declare that you will live a fulfilled and successful life. I declare that you will produce, multiply and replenish what God has given you. I declare that you are wealthy in your finances, in wisdom, in praises, in honor, in power, might, glory, and blessings. (Revelation 5:12) In the name of Jesus!

ABOUT THE AUTHOR

Lakisha Thomas is a wife and a mother of two children. She is a strong woman who believes that dreams can and will come true. She daily put forth her best effort to be the best mother and wife possible. She is the C.E.O and founder PLTM Ministries. She has a deep love for God and his kingdom. She has been serving in ministry since 2013. Her passion is to do the Father's work by healing the sick, delivering the captives, and preaching the gospel. Lakisha is a true believer in prayer and the ways of the kingdom. It doesn't have to make sense to humans if God said it, as long as He has said it, do it!